YOU CAN DO ANYTHING!
SUCCESS STORIES FOR KIDS

Contents

"Kid, You Should Probably Stick to Driving a Truck."

Rejection hurts. When people don't believe in you, that can hurt too. It might surprise you that most people who achieve anything have to overcome the disbelief of others (and themselves), even people being rude. This story is about a guy who became the biggest star in the world. For a long time, he was the most famous person on the planet. Yet, during one audition, he was told that he would never make it as a singer.

You may have heard of Elvis Presley. He was one of the first "rock and roll" singers. But it wasn't easy for him. His family was poor when he was young. He grew up in Mississippi, and his family needed help to get food to eat. They lost their home because they didn't have enough money when Elvis' dad was thrown in jail.

Elvis was always crazy about music. But that didn't make his life any easier at first. He was bullied at school and didn't have any friends. When he was 10 years old, he entered a school singing contest and came in 5th place. This wasn't terrible, but not great either. He started taking his guitar to school every day and singing songs. But his classmates just told him that he was "trashy" for playing what they called hillbilly music.

In the eighth grade, Elvis got a C in music class. His teacher had told him that he wasn't a very good singer. This made him mad. So he brought his guitar

in and sang a song in the class. The teacher was still not impressed and said that she "didn't appreciate his kind of singing." Elvis said that his music classes growing up were the only classes that he failed. That's not exactly a confidence booster!

By the time he was 16 years old, he was already working as a truck driver. Elvis wanted to be a singer more than anything. But he had no idea how to accomplish his goal. He lived in Memphis and hung out around record production studios but nobody thought he was very talented.

Elvis got a good job driving a truck for an electric company. But he was much more interested in music. One of his friends was a guy named Ronnie Smith. Ronnie was in a real band, so that impressed Elvis. The guy whose band Ronnie played in was Eddie Bond. Eddie was much older than Elvis and had been in the music business for over 20 years.

It just so happened that Eddie needed a singer for his new band. Ronnie told Elvis that he should try out for his dream job. Elvis was shy and did the best he could. This tryout was Elvis' first big chance. What he heard from Eddie was crushing. After singing a couple of songs, Eddie told the future king of rock and roll that he shouldn't quit his truck driver job "because you're never going to make it as a singer."

How rude is that? Poor Elvis! He must have walked out of there feeling terrible. Was his dream of being a singer a stupid one? He must have wanted to give up. But he had plenty of chances to give up before and hadn't. He decided not to let Eddie Bond make him quit either.

Just a couple of months after that happened, he managed to record a song at a real studio. This studio wasn't that interested in Elvis, but they let the kid try. It didn't go well. They played music all night and didn't have anything that the producer, Sam Philips, thought was any good. They were about to give up and go home.

Just then, Elvis grabbed a guitar. He sang a song called "That's All Right (Mama)" and started dancing around, acting silly, and having fun. The two other studio musicians liked it and started to play and dance silly also.

Sam stuck his head in and asked what they were doing. That was the sound he had been looking for! He told them to knock it off so he could start recording and told them to start over. Three days later that song was on the radio, and people were going crazy over it. Look it up, it's a catchy tune!

From that moment on, Elvis was unstoppable. He had never gotten any formal music training. He had no idea how to read music which is important for musicians. So many people who had heard him sing, thought he stunk! None of that mattered. Elvis could sing. He just had a whole new way of doing it that people hadn't heard before.

Elvis has still sold more albums than almost anybody with around 500 million records sold. He became a movie star too. He still has the record for the most hit songs...ever. He changed music forever with his new style of singing. And all of that only happened because he didn't listen to people who thought he wasn't any good. He kept believing in himself anyway. And by not giving up on his dreams, that poor "trashy" kid who wasn't supposed to make it, changed the world.

"When I was a child...I was a dreamer. I read comic books and I was the hero of the comic book. I saw movies and I was the hero in the movie. So every dream I ever dreamed has come true a hundred times..."

- Elvis Presley

The 15-Year-Old Janitor Who
Became a Superstar

What if I told you that there was a kid who had to live in a van when he was 12, dropped out of high school, and worked as a janitor cleaning poop when he was 15? How could this guy grow up to be one of the biggest comedy stars in the world and make movies that have earned nearly 5 billion dollars? Crazy, right?

The family was living in Ontario, Canada when the dad lost his job. They became homeless and lived out of their van or in a tent. That's a really hard life. They moved around a lot, and the parents did whatever they could for work. They finally got a job cleaning out a warehouse at night. The boy was 15 and dropped out of high school and worked as a janitor there. It was a gross job. Sometimes the kid got mad about his life and would punch holes in the walls. But sometimes he would feel okay and dance around dreaming and singing as he cleaned.

The boy dreamed of being a comedian. He was funny. It might work. That year his dad took him to a comedy club to get up and do his funny impressions. That's a really brave thing to do when you're 15! The audience hated it, and that was really embarrassing. But after another year, the boy's dad got a good job, and the family finally moved into a real house. Thank goodness. That made everything easier.

The boy was now 17 and wanted to try comedy again. He actually got a job performing for $20 a night. That was really great for his confidence. He even went back to the club where he had bombed so badly two years earlier. It wasn't so bad this time. He was getting better all the time and even auditioned to get on the TV show, Saturday Night Live. He wasn't chosen for the show but more than 20 years later he would be invited to be the celebrity host. But for now, it was back to more hard work.

When he was 19, he got a job as the opening act at a rock concert. The crowd hated him and booed loudly and yelled so much that he had to leave the stage. He was supposed to go back the next night but refused. It was around this time that he got his first big break. A newspaper writer had seen one of his acts and loved it. This nice write-up got him more jobs, and he even made it onto a TV show. As that year went on, he got more jobs, and people were noticing. He had built up a good reputation in Canada and was getting more opportunities. But this was difficult work and didn't pay much.

When the young comic was 21 years old, he moved to Hollywood, California and started performing in comedy clubs. He would bounce between there and Toronto, Canada for another nine years of struggle. Those years were full of hard work, rejections, and failure. But he had just enough success to keep going.

He would later say that in order to stay positive, he wrote himself a check for ten million dollars and carried it around in his pocket. He wrote on it that it was for "acting services". He would pretend that he had already been paid the ten million dollars. That helped him believe that he was on the right track and that things would eventually work out. He says the real key to all of his success was never giving up and putting in all of the hard work. He dated the check for three or five years in the future. It seemed impossible. But just before his date arrived that he wanted to be paid $10 million for acting in a movie, he found out that his impossible dream had come true. He was hired to be in a movie and he would get paid exactly ten million dollars!

Okay, who is this guy? I've been telling you about the early life of Jim Carrey, who you've probably seen play the Grinch in *How the Grinch Stole Christmas*. Or maybe you've seen him in one of his other big-hit movies. For most of his early life, Jim Carrey REALLY struggled. It was hard to grow up living on the streets during his early teens, and it takes a lot of guts and work to make it as a comedian. But he finally broke through and became the huge smash-hit superstar that we all know and love today.

After he became famous, Jim was invited to give a speech at a college graduation ceremony. He told the graduating students to try not to make their decisions in life based on fear. He said, "So many of us choose our path out of fear disguised as practicality. What we really want seems impossibly out of reach and ridic-ulous to expect. So we never dare to ask the universe for it. I'm saying I'm the proof that you can ask the universe for it."

What he meant is that we all tend not to have really big dreams. We choose fear or safety instead. He went on to say, "My father could have been a great comedian, but he didn't believe that that was possible for him. And so he made a conservative choice. Instead, he got a safe job as an accountant. And when I was 12 years old, he was let go from that safe job, and our family had to do whatever we could to survive. I learned many great lessons from my father, not the least of which was that you can fail at what you don't want so you might as well take a chance on doing what you love."

Jim really did learn that lesson when he was a kid. And it inspired him to go for his big dreams no matter what. Chasing big dreams can be scary. It can be hard to believe in yourself. But Jim kept going; he kept trying even when it was hard. That's what makes Jim Carrey's story so inspiring.

"It is better to risk starving to death than surrender. If you give up on your dreams, what's left?"

- Jim Carrey

A 16-Year-Old Waitress Did What??

I doubt you've ever heard of Julia Stewart. She's not a famous athlete or movie star, but she has accomplished something that is absolutely incredible. It all began when she was a 16-year-old girl getting one of her first jobs. She was a waitress at an IHOP restaurant. IHOP is short for International House of Pancakes. It's a restaurant that is known for serving lots of breakfast foods. Yum!

As a young waitress, Julia had a tough job. "My coffee is cold!" "I need more syrup!" "My baby spilled milk everywhere! Can we get some napkins?" These are all things she may have had to deal with. She had to be cheerful and call everyone sir or ma'am. Being a waitress is hard work! You take lots of orders and have to keep them all straight in your head and get them right. Your boss will be mad if you mess an order up.

Julia learned a lot in that job. And guess what? She LOVED it. She liked all of the action and energy that goes along with working in a restaurant. Her dad was really disappointed by this because he wanted her to be a teacher. But Julia was determined. She loved restaurants. She went to college where she studied advertising and selling. She even invented a small machine that made hamburgers in the shape of McDonald's golden arches. She called it the "McDonald's masher". That got picked up by a news station, and somebody offered her a job with an advertising company. Go Julia!

She worked in that business for fifteen years and became an important advertising boss. But she never forgot how fun it was to work in a restaurant. So she went back to it and became a boss at a Taco Bell. Her advertising co-workers thought she was crazy to leave that fancy job just to work in a Taco Bell. She had to work late at night and on the weekends and make sure the floors got mopped.

She stuck with it and kept getting promoted. She ended up being in charge of not just one Taco Bell but 5,600 of them! Julia was smart and a really hard worker. People liked her. After that job, she was hired to be in charge of every Applebee's restaurant in the United States. She was the President of a company now.

Julia wasn't like most restaurant company presidents. She had to visit all of the restaurants as the new president. So what did she do? She put on an Applebee's waitress uniform and started taking orders again and talking to customers. She didn't tell the customers that she was the company president. They thought she was an ordinary waitress. Julia learned a lot by doing that. She did such a good job at being the company's president that she was promised that she would be promoted again to the CEO.

The CEO is the boss of everyone in a company, even the company's president. But instead, the company hired someone else! Julia was not happy. So what did she do? This is Julia Stewart we're talking about. She left and became the CEO of the restaurant company that she first worked at when she was 16 years old. She was now the top boss of IHOP, the company where she used to clean ketchup bottles and take orders from customers. Now SHE was the one who gave out the orders.

The story gets even better. As the leader of the company that ran all the IHOP restaurants, she took over and bought the Applebee's company! When she did, she walked into the office of the guy who hadn't promoted her and fired him. Wow! Julia was now in charge of all the IHOPs AND all of the Applebee's restaurants. She was now running a company that made hundreds of millions of dollars each year and was worth billions. And she had started at the very beginning as a young girl filling up people's coffees.

"Believe in yourself and your abilities (while continuing to add to them and improve them)."

- Julia Stewart

From a Girl Who Couldn't Walk to the Fastest Woman in the World

This baby may not survive. She was born premature and only weighed a little over four pounds. That was especially dangerous in 1940 when she was born. But the baby lived. That was the good news. The bad news was that she was always getting sick. Scarlet fever nearly killed her. There was also a bout with measles and whooping cough. Then it was pneumonia. And after this sickly little girl had survived all of that, she caught polio. She was only 5 years old.

The girl was named Wilma, and she lived in Clarkesville, Tennessee. Her dad had a lot of kids. When she was born, she had nineteen older brothers and sisters. Luckily, Wilma lived through the polio like she had with all the other illnesses, but the disease had left her left leg and foot mostly useless. The only way that she could walk was with the help of a leg brace. That was really hard for a 5-year-old.

Poor Wilma would have to wear a brace for another seven years. Wilma's mom took her by bus on a fifty-mile trip to a hospital in Nashville where they would work on her leg. They did that every week for two years. Wilma needed her leg massaged every single day. This kid was a LOT of work for her mom and

family. She was always too sick to go to school. She even missed all of Kindergarten and the first grade.

When Wilma was 12, she could finally walk on her own. And soon after that, she was in middle school discovering sports. Not only could Wilma walk, she could run too! Wilma found out that she was an incredible athlete. And after all of those years of being sick and not being able to walk, this was fun. Running was really fun.

Her high school basketball coach nicknamed her "Skeeter" because she was as fast as a mosquito. When she was in the 10th grade, she set a school record for the most points scored during a basketball season. She also enjoyed running for the track team. A college track coach saw one of her basketball games when she was 14 and could tell that Wilma was special. He invited her to his track camp and then took her to a track event in Pennsylvania. Wilma ran in nine events. And Wilma won nine events. This kid was on her way, and everyone knew it. Skeeter was going places.

When Wilma was only 16 years old, she qualified for the Olympics. She went to Australia and won a bronze medal in a relay with three other women. Wilma was the youngest Olympian to represent the United States at that Olympics. Not many high schoolers get that chance. Her fellow classmates back home were all really impressed with her medal and loved to hold it. But Wilma wanted gold. She would get her chance four years later.

Wilma was now 20 years old and in college when she would get her chance at the next Olympics. This time they were in Rome, Italy. Wilma had already set a new world record for the fastest 200-meter dash at the Olympic tryouts. Everyone knew that this girl from Clarkesville had a chance at winning gold.

But no American woman had won the 100-meter dash at the Olympics for more than 20 years. Could this 20-year-old kid really do it? 1960 was the first year that the Olympics were on television. The whole world was watching. And what they saw was Wilma Rudolph become an international superstar.

She won the 100-meter dash with the fastest time in history. Then she won the 200-meter dash with another world record. That was two gold medals and two world records. Then it was time for the relay, the event that she had won a bronze medal in four years earlier. Wilma was the anchor, the fourth team member to run. When she crossed the finish line, it would be over. Her three teammates were all fellow college students and teammates with her at Tennessee State University. It was them against the world.

They set a new world record in the semifinals. But in the final race for the gold, Wilma almost dropped the baton during the handoff! She was now behind the German runner and would have to catch up. The whole world looked on as she ran so fast that she passed the German runner right at the finish line to win a third gold medal for the United States.

Newspapers all over the world called Wilma, "The Tornado, the fastest woman on earth." She became one of the biggest stars of the 1960 Olympics. The whole world was talking about her with millions of people watching it all happen. No American woman had ever won that many gold medals at one Olympics. Her mother was so proud. All of those trips to the hospital and daily care had led to this unimaginable moment. Wilma Rudolph, the girl who couldn't even walk for seven years growing up, had become the fastest woman in the world. There is nothing that we can't overcome if we believe in ourselves and keep working.

"Never Underestimate the Power of Dreams and the Influence of the Human Spirit."
- Wilma Rudolph

Fired for a Lack of Imagination, His Big Ideas Changed the World

Have you ever been to Disney World or Disneyland? They're amazing, right? They were created by one incredibly creative man, Walt Disney. He dreamed it all up. But when he was 18 years old and just starting his career, he was fired.

Walt worked as a cartoonist at a newspaper, the Kansas City Star. And that is what he had always wanted to do. It all started when Walt was just 5 years old. He would copy all of the cartoons from the newspaper. He drew and drew, and then drew some more. He loved it more than anything. And he would be hooked on cartoons for the rest of his life.

Back in 1910, it was common for kids to work. As a 10-year-old, Walt started his first job. He delivered newspapers every morning. He had to wake up at 4:30 a.m. to do that job. The newspaper had to be delivered every day. And Walt kept up that job (and early morning schedule) for six years! And what was the paper that he delivered? It was the Kansas City Star.

Waking up that early every day wasn't easy. It made it hard to do well in school. Walt was always getting in trouble for falling asleep during class. (I'll bet that would make your teachers pretty upset too.) So Walt wasn't the best student, and his grades were not very

good. But that was okay with him. All he cared about was drawing cartoons.

When Walt started high school, he (of course) worked as the cartoonist for the school paper. He also took night classes at a nearby art school. Walt loved his country and decided that he wanted to go fight in World War I. The year was 1918, and the war had been going on for a few years. Walt was only 16, which was too young to join the army, so they turned him away. I'll show them, he thought. Walt changed the date on his birth certificate to a year earlier to make it seem like he was older than he was and joined the Red Cross as an ambulance driver. He was barely old enough to drive!

He ended up in France but didn't have to stay long because the war ended shortly after he got there. But Walt was able to get his cartoons into the army news-paper and even drew cartoons on the side of his ambu-lance. He just couldn't help himself.

He moved back home to Kansas City and was thrilled to get a job once again, working for the Kan-sas City Star just like he had done as a kid. Only this time he wasn't delivering the papers...he had gotten his dream job of drawing the cartoons in them. Unfortu-nately, Walt's editor wasn't very impressed with him. He told Walt that he "lacked imagination and had no good ideas." He was fired.

What?!? This is Walt Disney we're talking about! As you might guess, Walt Disney wasn't the kind of guy to let that stop him. And it's a good thing because that would mean a world without those amazing theme parks and movies. Walt would need a lot of determination, though.

He started his own cartoon company with a friend of his. It only lasted a month because they couldn't get enough customers. He started to learn animation, which was the process of taking still cartoons and making them into a moving cartoon or short movie. He started a new company making animated cartoons or short cartoon movies. And it started to work.

He got customers. So he hired people and was having lots of fun. But after a couple of years, that company ran out of money also. That was business failure number two.

That was when the dejected 21-one-year-old Walt Disney moved from Kansas to Hollywood, California. Actually, it's not that clear that Walt was dejected. He simply kept trying. He had a twelve-minute animation of Alice in Wonderland that he had created. He was determined to sell it to a studio in Hollywood. He got lots and lots of "No thank you's".

But then he got a "Yes"! There was one movie distributor who needed a new cartoon series. Two years after moving to Hollywood, Walt was in business with a new company. He called his new business, Walt Disney Studio.

A couple of years later, he created the iconic Mickey Mouse, and the world would never be the same. Walt Disney would go on to win 22 Academy Awards and be nominated an astounding 59 times. Those are the big awards given out in the movie industry. The next closest individual winner has 5 Academy Awards. Walt Disney's record number of awards will probably never be broken.

Walt Disney's company now makes nearly $90 billion every single year. Creating the Disneyland and Disney World theme parks filled him with joy. He loved watching kids run through the parks full of excitement and happiness. Walt became regarded as one of the most forward-thinking, brilliantly creative people ever. Unlike what he was told by that newspaper editor when he was young, not only did he have great imagination, he may have had more good ideas than anybody in history! His story illustrates (as so many do) how important it is to believe in yourself even when other people don't.

**"All our dreams can come true,
if we have the courage to pursue them."
- Walt Disney**

For All the "Weirdos"

This story is for you if you have ever been made fun of for how you look. And just so you know, we have all been made fun of for our appearance at some point. This story is also for you if people think you're weird in any way. It's also for you if you've been tempted to think that other kids are weird. They might be the ones to become famous someday!

In a little town in the north of England, there was born a boy who didn't look like everyone else. He didn't act like everyone else. He didn't speak like everyone else. His name was Rowan. The other kids at his school thought he looked like an alien because his face looked strange. Poor Rowan also had a speech impediment. Rowan stuttered.

Stuttering makes it hard to talk. Rowan knew what he wanted to say, but his stuttering made it hard for him to get the words out. Lots of people have this speech problem, and it usually makes people shy, awkward, and very unsure of themselves.

Rowan was bullied. Not many of the other kids were nice to him at all. That makes it really hard to be excited to go to school. Kids like Rowan dread it. Every day is scary when you're being bullied. But there was one thing that Rowan liked about school, and that was science.

His science classes were his favorite. Rowan thought that he might be a scientist one day. One of

his teachers wasn't so sure. They said, "Nothing is outstanding about him. I don't expect him to become a fantastic scientist."

It wasn't just that teacher that didn't believe in Rowan, nobody seemed to. So it was probably a big shock when Rowan was accepted into one of the most fancy colleges in England, Oxford University. College is a great chance to start fresh for kids who aren't popular or well-liked where they're from. It was in college that Rowan realized how much he enjoyed... acting?

He still had his speech impediment, but he went for it anyway. And the really shocking thing? Acting was fun! Rowan especially liked being silly on stage and being in comedies. But because he stuttered, he told himself that being a professional actor must be a silly dream for someone like him.

Rowan got a master's degree in electrical engineering. But acting was still calling to him. He had put so much work and money into studying science. Could he just throw that away for something he enjoyed more when that thing was being silly and making people laugh?

It can be really hard for people to choose to chase their passions and dreams over a more reasonable or practical path. But Rowan made the brave choice. Or was it crazy?

He joined a comedy group. His speech impediment made things difficult for him. He tried out for roles on television shows. Rejection. Rowan didn't just have to overcome stuttering but casting directors thought that he also looked a little weird for television.

Rowan refused to give up. He discovered that whenever he was playing a character that he had made up for himself, his stutter went away. So he started writing his own comedy. Could this work?

It could. And it did. Rowan started to get work. First on radio and then on television! He got more and more popular. He created a funny character called Blackadder that became quite popular. People in England loved that show. But superstardom was just around the corner.

Rowan created a new character. He called him Mr. Bean. Mr. Bean was extremely silly...and strange. People LOVED it. This new character was a smash hit. Rowan started to earn millions of dollars for the TV shows and movies that he was writing and starring in.

Rowan Atkinson is now worth around $150 million from his acting career. He is still a giant comedy star and has even been in a James Bond movie. You've probably heard his voice before. Have you seen the original Lion King? Rowan was the voice of Zazu, the funny bird who worked for both Mufasa and Simba.

No matter how strange people think you are because of things that you can't help, you are capable of great things. It takes believing in yourself and lots of hard work. It also takes lots of courage and determination. But Rowan's story proves that anyone who wants it bad enough can achieve their dreams. I'll bet his class bullies feel really bad about how they treated him now!

"To be successful, you don't need a beautiful face and heroic body. What you need is a skillful mind and ability to perform."

- Rowan Atkinson

Who on Earth Is Silence Dogood?

You're about to find out something really wild about one of the most important people in American history. I think you'll find it really funny. There's a lot that you may not know about Benjamin Franklin.

Did you know that he dropped out of school when he was 10? If you don't feel like going to school one day, just try that one out on your mom or dad. I have a hunch that even though things worked out for Benjamin, it probably won't get you out of school.

Benjamin didn't drop out of school because he wanted to. His family ran out of money. When Benjamin was a kid, school wasn't free like it is today. Benjamin didn't seem to care. It was as if he already knew that he was destined for the history books anyway. He would just teach himself. His father had wanted him to be a preacher, and that didn't sound like much fun to Benjamin. He wanted to escape out to sea and live a life of adventure.

In the meantime, Benjamin read and read and read. He learned all kinds of stuff when he wasn't working for his dad in his soap business. You might say that he was mostly self-taught. He thought that making soap was really boring. He'd rather read and write. When he was 12, he worked for his older brother. And that's when things get pretty funny.

James was Benjamin's older brother, and he worked in printing. Printing was big business in those days. Books, newspapers, they all needed printing. And nobody had smartphones or televisions so they all wanted to read the paper every day. Benjamin started writing poetry and enjoyed it. But his father didn't like that one bit and told him that, "Verse-makers were generally beggars." Benjamin kept writing anyway.

James started his own newspaper when Benjamin was 15. That was great news. Benjamin figured that his brother would surely let him be a writer for the new paper. But James said, "No thanks, little brother. If you really want to be useful, sweep the floor!" At least that's how I imagine it. But it's clear that James didn't think that a 15-year-old had any business writing for a serious newspaper.

But Benjamin really wanted this. So he came up with a clever plan. He began slipping articles underneath the door of the newspaper at night. He signed the articles that he wrote with the name "Silence Dogood". Isn't that a funny name? He said that he was a middle-aged lady with strong opinions about current events. He even disguised his handwriting.

It worked! James liked them and published them. These articles by the mysterious Silence Dogood became extremely popular. People really enjoyed the writing and looked forward to reading more. The articles became a bit of a sensation in Boston. Everyone wondered who this lady really was.

After many weeks and 14 articles by Silence Dogood had been published, Benjamin must not have been able to hold it in any longer. He proudly told James that it was him who was the real Silence Dogood. James was angry that he had been tricked. He was also jealous that the letters had gotten so much attention.

Benjamin finally had enough of working for his older brother and ran away to New York where he could do as he pleased. But life was hard for runaways. He failed to find a job as a printer and went down to Philadelphia hoping for better luck. He got off the boat and used the last of his money to buy some bread. He just might end up a beggar as his father had warned him.

With no money in his pockets, the clever Benjamin did find a job in his new town as a printer. That was a close one! It would be the last time that he was ever penniless. From that moment on, the path of Benjamin's life was one of success and wealth. Years later (when he wasn't flying kites in lightning storms) he was elected to the second Continental Congress and joined the movement for American independence from England.

You probably know how the rest of his story goes and that he was a signer of the Declaration of Independence. But I think how he tricked his brother and took a chance on carving out his own path in life is really fun to learn about. It's also key to his character. It's no wonder that he became an important figure in America's fight for independence. Benjamin had already fought for his own independence in life all those years earlier when he ran away from his brother in Boston.

People who aren't brave and do what everyone else tells them to usually don't make it into history books. Benjamin Franklin was one of history's great rebels.

"Do not fear mistakes. You will know failure. Continue to reach out." "Motivation is when your dreams put on work clothes."
- Benjamin Franklin

The Foster Kid Who Ignored His Teachers' Advice

Growing up without parents is really hard. Unfortunately, lots and lots of kids have to do it. That's the situation that young Paul Williams found himself in. The year was 1898, not that long after the American Civil War. Paul lived in Los Angeles, California, and both of his parents had died from a disease called tuberculosis. Paul was only 4 years old and he was alone.

Paul lived with foster families, who are wonderful people that take children into their homes when they have no other place to go. Paul got lucky and got to live with a really nice couple who did all they could for him, and they lived in a nice place. But Paul was a bit out of place there. Paul was Black, and the neighborhood that his foster family lived in was mostly White. Paul was the only Black kid in his entire elementary school. But even though it was the early 1900s, Paul wasn't made to feel bad about it. He later said that everyone treated him very well.

He fell in love with architecture, which is the design of buildings and houses. And his foster mother always told him that he could do anything he wanted when he grew up and be anything that he wanted to be. It might be that he wanted to design homes because he never had his own when he was young. But there was

one problem with what Paul wanted to be. There were absolutely no Black architects anywhere. Lots of people didn't think that Black people were as smart as White people. Paul's high school guidance counselor couldn't believe it when Paul told them what he wanted to do. They said to him, "Whoever heard of a Black person being an architect?"

Paul didn't care. He wrote later about how he felt about that guidance counselor's reaction to his dreams. "If I allow the fact that I am Black to checkmate my will to do, now, I will inevitably form the habit of being defeated." Paul decided that nothing was going to stop him, not racism, not anything. He would NOT be defeated. It didn't matter to him that there weren't any other Black architects. He would be the first. Another teacher told him that White people would never hire a Black architect. Paul didn't care about that either. He said, "I owe it to myself and to my people to accept this challenge."

Paul got to work on his craft with a new determination. When he graduated high school, he went to every architect firm in Los Angeles looking for work. Three of them offered him the job of "errand boy". But Paul had no interest in running errands. One firm offered him an internship. He wouldn't be paid. He would have to work for free and prove himself.

And Paul did exactly that. The firm didn't take long to decide to pay him. Paul would go to work and at night he would go to engineering school. He eventually earned a college degree. He was now a certified architect. Just two years later, Paul was able to start his own company. It was 1920 and the population of Los Angeles was starting to explode. People needed houses, and Paul was too good to ignore. Over the next 20 years, he would design almost 3,000 spectacular homes.

After all of that work, Paul kept getting better and better jobs. He became the architect of choice for Hollywood's stars, designing houses for the city's most famous and richest people. But it was important to Paul to also do work designing churches and housing projects. He also designed iconic buildings all over the country like St. Jude's Children's Hospital in Memphis, Tennessee.

Paul became one of the best architects in the entire world. And he did that despite being told that it would never work and that he would never get hired. Paul Williams epitomized the courage it takes to follow your dreams even when others tell you that you can't.

"Without having the wish to 'show them,' I developed a fierce desire to 'show myself.' I wanted to vindicate every ability I had. I wanted to acquire new abilities. I wanted to prove that I, AS AN INDIVIDUAL, deserved a place in the world."

- Paul Williams

The Peasant Boy Whose Destiny
Was to Save the World

They were trapped. The air conditioning was no longer working on the submarine. The men were drenched with sweat. They had been down there for days and were running out of air. The radio, which connected them to base, wasn't working either. The warships above had dropped depth charges. These were bombs sinking through the water, getting closer by the second.

They might be moments away from dying at the bottom of the ocean. All around him, men were panicking and shouting about the explosions they could hear up above them. Unknown to the men on the ships at the surface, in the submarine's torpedo hold was a nuclear warhead. It had the power to completely destroy a city the size of Miami, Florida, and start a nuclear war. And the captain was screaming for them to fire.

I'm describing what many historians call the most dangerous moment in all of human history. That's not an exaggeration. The United States and the Soviet Union were on the edge of a full-on nuclear war. If both countries fired their nuclear missiles at each other, nearly everyone in North America and Russia could have died. The calm thinking of one man kept this from happening. The story of how he got to that submarine in that moment in history is a remarkable one.

It was cold that January. But that wasn't unusual. It was Russia. The year was 1926. A boy was born to a peasant woman in the little river town of Staraya Kupavna. Russian peasants at that time lived in complete poverty, making their living off of what they could grow. A harsh winter could mean starving. That was how Vasily Arkhipov grew up. It was how most Russians grew up in the 1920s and 30s. But most Russians wouldn't grow up to save the world.

When Vasily was 16, he could either keep farming as his father was doing or he could join the army. Vasily enlisted in naval school. Anything had to be better than scraping by growing cabbages. The young man was smart and did well in school. But he had to take a break from his studies when he was 19 to serve in World War II. He worked onboard a boat called a minesweeper. Two years later he graduated from a higher naval school which prepared him for a military career.

He joined the Russian navy right out of school and found himself on submarines working in the cold seas all around the Soviet Union. When Vasily was 34, he was promoted to deputy commander on a sleek new nuclear submarine. Its first voyage was to the north Atlantic Ocean, near Greenland. There was no backup system on the submarine and it wasn't made very well. The crew was in trouble. The cooling system failed which might mean a complete nuclear meltdown and disaster.

This meant that the whole crew was in danger as well as the entire Atlantic Ocean. The radio went out. The crew was on their own. They would have to act fast to avoid an environmental catastrophe. This was just the first nuclear mess that Vasily found himself in the middle of. He had to work hard to prevent a mutiny and keep everyone calm while the engineering crew gave their lives to fix the problem. Those seven men died working on the reactor. They were exposed to the radiation for too long. But the submarine was able to get back home safely.

Just over a year later, the world would nearly see the beginning of a nuclear war. This was called the Cuban Missile Crisis. Four Soviet nuclear submarines were in the water around Cuba, which is less than 300 miles from Florida. They were ordered to hide by their Soviet commanders. Then they lost contact. Days later, Vasily's submarine was found by a group of US warships.

The US navy wanted the submarine to come to the surface so they could talk. They dropped practice depth charges to get the submarine's attention. The Soviet Union and the United States had been on the brink of war before the submarine lost contact with their naval command back in Moscow. For all they knew, they were now at war.

The US destroyer dropped "signaling" depth charges. These exploded but were not intended to sink the submarine. The navy captain on the destroyer thought that this would convince the submarine to come to the surface. Instead, it convinced the submarine captain that they were at war. The captain panicked and ordered the nuclear torpedo to be fired.

But he needed the approval of the other two officers on board. Everyone was screaming. The other officer agreed that they were about to die and they might as well obliterate the boat that was about to kill them. It all came down to Vasily. His captain yelled, "We're gonna blast them now! We will die, but we will sink them all. We will not become the shame of the fleet." But thankfully, Vasily remained calm.

Vasily had already survived a near nuclear catastrophe a year earlier. That experience must have helped to keep him level headed. He was also very respected because of the courage he showed during that emergency. He was able to calm his captain down and convince him to surface. They would engage with the US destroyer and try to get new commands from Moscow by getting the radio working on the surface.

Had the decision to launch the nuclear warhead been only up to Vasily's captain, it would not have taken long for the generals and the president of the United States to find out that their destroyer had been blown up by a Soviet submarine. It would have meant war. It would have meant the launch of nuclear missiles toward the Soviet Union and toward the United States. Death would have been everywhere.

Thanks to the decision of one man in the midst of the most intense and stressful of situations, nuclear war did not happen. Not many people know the name of Vasily Arkhipov. But all Americans and all Russians probably owe him for our being alive today. That's a pretty great achievement for a kid who was born into poverty in the Russian countryside.

"(My father) always thought that he did what he had to do and never considered his actions as heroism. He did his part for the future so that everyone can live on our planet."
- Elena Andriukova, Vasily Arkhipov's daughter

How an Angry Boy Became an International Superstar

I love looking back on the lives of successful people. It's easy to forget that they had no idea that they would become successful. The legend of Bruce Lee is one such story. It's full of rejection and failure. He could have easily spent his life never amounting to much. But he decided that his destiny would be one of glory and success. And that's exactly what happened. He grew up to be the most famous martial artist in the world and a famous actor. But it wasn't easy.

Bruce had a good childhood. His dad was a celebrity where they lived in Hong Kong, which is a region of China. Bruce's dad was an opera singer. Everyone knew who he was. And as a great singer, he was in lots of movies. This meant that Bruce grew up around the movie scene in Hong Kong. He was actually in one as a baby!

When Bruce was just 9 years old he got the chance to have the lead role in a movie with his dad. By the time that Bruce was 18, he had acted in 20 movies. He was a busy kid! But he wasn't the best student at school and always seemed to be getting into trouble. Bruce had learned boxing and was getting into fights. His parents were disappointed by this and decided to get him some different training.

Bruce's dad worked hard to get him accepted into a special martial arts training school. It was run by a famous master called Yip Man. Bruce did well there and was lucky enough to be one of the few students to be trained personally by Yip Man himself. Yip Man didn't want his students fighting in the streets. He taught discipline. Bruce loved it and soaked up everything he could.

But the fighting gangs on the streets of Hong Kong would find Bruce. He started getting into lots of fights. After one bad fight on a rooftop, Bruce was arrested. His mom had to go get him out of jail and decided that she needed to get him out of Hong Kong. Bruce was in high school when he was sent to San Francisco, California, to live with his older sister. His parents didn't want him fighting dangerous Chinese gangs and thought that America would be safer for him.

They were right. Bruce kept training in Karate and Kung Fu. He was one of the best around. He could do pushups on the tips of two of his fingers. Yip Man had taught him the one-inch punch. Bruce could hold his hand and not swing his arm to punch. His fist only went one inch but was so powerful that it would knock other fighters to the floor.

Then Hollywood came calling for Bruce. He got a big break to be on a popular television show, The Green Hornet. Bruce would play the hero's sidekick, Kato. This was Bruce's first job performing in the United States and people loved the show. The director wanted him to fight like other actors but Bruce refused. He had his own style that he'd been using his whole life. He wasn't going to change now. Bruce was actually so fast that his karate moves couldn't be picked up by the camera. He had to slow down his movement so that viewers could see his character's punches and kicks.

He worked odd jobs on movies and TV shows for several years after that. He pitched his idea for a TV show that he would be the star in to a big studio but was rejected. His idea was stolen and another actor cast in the lead role. Bruce was only 20 years old. His acting career seemed to be at a dead end. Hollywood didn't seem ready for Asian movie stars. But Bruce was determined. He decided to write down his goals on a piece of paper.

It was 1961 when he wrote, "I, Bruce Lee, will be the first highest-paid Oriental superstar in the United States. In return, I will give the most exciting performances and render the best of quality in the capacity of an actor. Starting 1970 I will achieve world fame and from then onward till the end of 1980 I will have in my possession $10,000,000. I will live the way I please and achieve inner harmony and happiness."

Bruce decided to go back to Hong Kong to star in some movies there. Hollywood didn't seem ready for him to be the main star in a movie. This decision would make him an international superstar. His first leading role was in a Kung Fu movie called *The Big Boss*. Then he made *Fists of Fury*. Hollywood studios wanted him now and Bruce was doing what he loved.

Bruce started his own movie company and would now write, direct, and star in his own movies. He would be in complete control. He made the movie, *The Way of the Dragon*. Bruce cast a young karate champion as a villain that he had met back in California. His name was Chuck Norris. Bruce Lee gave Chuck his first big break and Chuck would go on to be a big Hollywood superstar thanks to this. Lots of movie critics have called the final showdown in that movie one of the best fight scenes in movie history.

The Way of the Dragon was a smash hit that earned tens of millions of dollars around the world. But it was Bruce's next movie, *Enter the Dragon*, that made martial arts mainstream in popular culture. *Enter the Dragon* made an astounding 400 million dollars in 1973. That would be around two *billion* dollars today. Bruce had accomplished his goal that he had written down all those years earlier. He was an international superstar who everyone loved and admired.

Tragically, Bruce would die that same year when he was only 32 years old. He had a rare allergic reaction to some medicine that killed him. People around the world were shocked and heartbroken. Bruce Lee had become a massively influential and important person. He studied philosophy and was universally admired for his wisdom. He knocked down barriers by changing how Asian people were portrayed in movies and television shows. Bruce was a hero to people everywhere. He did it by believing in himself and doing things his way.

"When I look around, I always learn something, and that is to be always yourself. And to express yourself. To have faith in yourself. Do not go out and look for a successful personality and duplicate it, which seems to me to be the prevalent thing happening...they always copy mannerisms, but they'll never start from the very root of being, which is 'how can I be me?'"

- Bruce Lee

A Dying Woman's Big Dream

It takes a lot of courage to chase your dreams. This is the story of a woman who knew that her chances were running out. It was now or never. Even though her dream was a simple one, it would not be easy. All she wanted was to see the Pacific Ocean before she died. In order to do that, she would have to ride a horse seven thousand miles.

Most people called Mesannie Wilkins "Annie." Annie was 63 years old and had just gotten some terrible news. Her doctor told her that she had two years to live. The spot that was on Annie's lung meant that she wouldn't live much longer. The doctor recommended that she take it easy in a retirement home. But that wasn't Annie's style.

Annie had a tough life. She grew up on a farm in a tiny town in Maine called Minot. She stopped going to school after the 6th grade to help do chores on the farm. As soon as she was old enough, she ran away and joined the circus. She did tricks on horses. But when she got word that her mom was sick, she went back home to help.

Annie's dad had died years earlier. The farm was struggling. Then her mom died. This was a really difficult time for Annie. Her mom's boyfriend was called Uncle Waldo. He stayed at the farm and did his best to help Annie keep it going.

Annie got a job in town but she didn't have a car so she rode an old mule to work. Annie and Waldo carried on for many years after her mom died. Then a terrible blizzard hit Maine. Annie caught pneumonia and was taken to the hospital. Waldo died while she was there. He was 85.

Annie had to sell everything to pay the hospital bills but she recovered, mostly. She was 63 and had just gotten the news from her doctor that she would be dead in two years because of the cancer on her lung. She was now all alone with just her dog, her farm, and a dream.

All that Annie could think about was her mom working so hard on that farm and how she always said that one day she would go see the Pacific Ocean. Her mom never did pull it off. She never saw it before she died. Annie decided that wouldn't happen to her. She would do what her mom couldn't. She would do this for her mom. Nothing else mattered.

Annie took out a loan on the family farm. The farm wasn't worth much but this got her some money so that she could buy a horse. She found a racehorse that was retired. His name was Tarzan and he was a beauty. Off they went. Annie, Tarzan, and her dog, Depeche Toi. That meant "hurry up" in French. Depeche Toi loved Annie and wouldn't be left behind.

Annie rolled up some clothes and off they went. This was crazy. Annie had to use all of her money to buy Tarzan. She would have to rely completely on the kindness of strangers. But people are kind, especially to a 63-year-old lady on a quest with just her horse and her dog.

When Depeche Toi got tired, he would ride with Annie on Tarzan. Other times he would happily run around on the end of her old clothesline as a leash. People gave her and her animal companions food as they went. They loved Annie's story. Hotels would let her stay for free. Police officers in small towns opened up a jail cell for her to get out of the weather. People let her spend the night on their farms and gave her money to help her along the journey. One farmer in Tennessee even gave her an extra horse named Rex to help carry the few things that she had and give Tarzan a break from time to time.

Annie rode along the highway and old country roads. She crossed rivers and mountains. She rode through storms and all kinds of weather. She made it as far as Arkansas where one man asked her to marry him. But Annie wouldn't be distracted from her mission.

Annie was a country girl and didn't realize how big the cities were and how much traffic she would have to deal with. Tarzan and Rex didn't like the loud noises and all the cars in the big cities. Depeche Toi didn't either.

Annie worried about her companions and her own health. Would it hold up long enough for her to make it? Exactly one year and twenty-three days after leaving her farm, Annie and her little caravan wandered into Redding, California, in December of 1955. She had done it!

She stood on the beach and stared in awe. It was the most beautiful thing she had ever seen. Full of accomplishment and happiness, she cried. She said a prayer for her mom and wished that she could be there too.

When Annie started her quest, she didn't know if she would make it. She had no money and would need lots of help. She felt sorry for herself, and the people back home in Maine had made fun of her.

But as she traveled, a funny thing happened. People told her how inspiring she was, and she saw the shock on people's faces when they found out what she was doing. She started to feel good about herself for the first time in years...maybe ever!

Journalists interviewed her and published her story in newspapers across the country. People lined up to meet her and get her autograph. Teachers asked her to speak to their classrooms and tell children about her inspiring story. She had never gotten so much attention in all her life.

And you know what? Annie WAS special! She told one interviewer that it was the best thing she had ever done. She remained in California for a couple of years. Annie was a celebrity now. People loved her story.

Wait. How was she still alive? Do you remember her cancer? Her doctor had been wrong! Annie was completely healthy. When she went back to Maine to visit, she went back in style. She was no longer broke, she had fancy clothes, and didn't need to ride a horse to get everywhere. The people back home didn't recognize her. Her return was a celebration. Annie even decided to write a book about her quest and became a published author. She went on to live for another glorious and adventure-filled 22 years.

Annie had been told to check into a retirement home and wait to die. Instead, she went on the adventure of a lifetime.

**"That's the thing about the future.
You can't get there by imagining. You can only get there one step at a time, and the hardest part is taking that first step."**

- Annie Wilkins

"You're How Old? Okay, Want a Job?"

There is one guy whose invention has changed everything about how people live today. I'm talking about the smartphone, or more specifically, Apple's iPhone. The story of the guy behind it is a fascinating one. His name was Steve Jobs, and you won't believe what he did as a 12-year-old...

Steve Jobs is one of the most influential geniuses of the past 100 years. The impact he had on our society is massive. So it might surprise you that he was a kid that nobody wanted.

Steve's real parents gave him up for adoption right away. He was offered to a couple who were looking to adopt, but they wanted a girl. They said no to Steve. He ended up being adopted by a couple who would love him very much. But his new mother thought that they might have made a really big mistake by adopting Steve.

His adoptive mother said, "Steve was so difficult a child that by the time he was two, I felt we had made a mistake. I wanted to return him." But she loved him fiercely, and his new parents did all they could for their new child. But Steve didn't make it easy on them.

Steve was smart, so he got bored easily in his elementary school classes. He turned into a prankster and was always getting into lots of trouble. He finally got

a wonderful teacher in the 5th grade who was able to get Steve interested and excited about learning things. He would carry that interest in learning for the rest of his life.

But things got bad again in middle school. Bullies! He was the new kid in the 6th grade, and that's never easy. Most of the other kids didn't like him very much and were mean to him. Bullies never think about how the kids they treat badly may grow up to be super successful or some of the wealthiest people in the world.

The bullying got so bad that in the middle of the 7th grade, Steve had enough. He told his parents that he was done with his middle school. He would drop out if they didn't move him to another school. Sometimes the answer is to tough it out. But the bullying was really bad for Steve. His parents knew he was serious.

So they spent all the money they had to get a new house in a better school district. The house they bought is now considered a historic site because the garage is where Steve built his first computer. His sister still owns the house to this day. The move had worked out for Steve, and he was much happier. He was now 12 years old, and life was about to get really interesting.

When Steve set his mind on something, he didn't let much get in his way. A couple of years earlier, Steve had started having fun taking different kinds of electronics apart and rebuilding them. He became friends with several engineers who lived in the neighborhood and learned from them.

Now that Steve was 12, he wanted to build a frequency counter. That's a machine that measures the number of pulses (or frequency) per second in electricity. To build such a machine, he needed special parts. How would a 12-year-old get these parts? For Steve, the answer was simple. He'd just call up the founder and CEO of a big computer company and ask!

HP Computers is still a really big company. HP stands for Hewlett-Packard, named after the two guys who started the company. Bill Hewlett was listed in the phone book. So Steve just gave him a call, and Bill answered! Steve told him his age and what he was trying to do. He then asked Bill if he could give him the parts he needed to build a frequency counter.

Bill laughed and thought it was pretty great to get a phone call from a 12-year-old about this. Bill's company actually built frequency counters. So his answer was yes. Of course, he would give this interesting kid the parts he needed. Would you like a summer job too? Steve said yes. (He lived in the same town that the company was in.) That next summer, a 13-year-old Steve worked on the assembly line that built frequency counters at HP Computers.

And that really set Steve Jobs on his way. When he grew up, he started his own computer company, Apple. Today, Apple is the most valuable company in the world, valued at nearly three trillion dollars. Lots of people buy Apple's MacBook computers, and it seems that nearly everyone has an Apple iPhone. And all that was started by an adopted kid who needed a home and wasn't afraid to ask for what he wanted.

"Most people never pick up the phone and ask and that's what separates the people who do things, and the people who just dream about them. <u>You gotta act.</u> You gotta be willing to fail. You gotta be willing to crash and burn. If you're afraid of failing, you won't get very far."

- Steve Jobs

I'd Rather Wrestle Grizzly Bears

It's hard to move to a different country where you don't really know anyone. It's even harder when you don't speak the language. But that's exactly what Rose Blumkin did when she moved from a little village in Belarus (a country in Eastern Europe) to join her husband in Iowa. Rose was 24 years old.

Rose traveled by herself to Seattle. Her husband had come ahead of her. She didn't know a single word of English. But she made it all the way to Iowa to be with her husband anyway. Together, they settled in Omaha, Nebraska, where they started a store selling used clothing.

Rose had grown up working in her parent's grocery store back in Belarus. When she was just 16, she became a manager and had 6 men reporting to her. She was born to be a businesswoman. Rose and her husband started a family, and when the children were older, they started a new venture. Rose borrowed $500 from her brother to get started.

The year was 1937. The United States was still in the Great Depression, which was probably a terrible time to start a business. People didn't have much money. But Rose was in her mid-forties, and she was ready. She started the Nebraska Furniture Mart, which sold used furniture. People were probably more likely to buy used furniture than new furniture when money

was scarce. But not many people were buying anything that they didn't have to in those days.

People really liked Rose. Most people called her Mrs. B. Word began to spread that she was the best person in the state to buy furniture from. Mrs. B ran her business with a simple motto. It was, "Sell cheap, tell the truth, don't cheat nobody." Customers loved it and came from all around to buy furniture from her.

The Nebraska Furniture Mart was growing fast. It became the biggest indoor furniture store in the entire United States. There was something really lucky about Mrs. B starting her business in Omaha, Nebraska. There was someone else who lived there that is very famous. He is one of the richest men in the world. His name is Warren Buffet, and he was a customer of Mrs. B.

Warren loved buying businesses. He still does. In 1983, Mrs. B was 90 years old. Warren said that when thinking about buying someone's business, he asks himself a question. Would he want to compete with that business, or would it be better to buy it? When it came to Mrs. B, he said, "I'd rather wrestle grizzlies than compete with Mrs. B and her (children)." He said that the Nebraska Furniture Mart was such a good business that there was no way to compete with it. He was right. So he bought it.

Mrs. B sold 90% of the company to Warren for $60 million. That's not bad for a girl who moved to the country without any money and couldn't even speak the language. That was an especially big amount of money back in 1983. Here's where the story gets even better.

Mrs. B worked there for another 5 years. Do you know any 95-year-olds who still work? Mrs. B had no interest in just sitting around. Usually, when one business buys another, they make the person who sells the business promise not to open a new business to compete with the business that they just sold. Warren always makes whoever he buys a business from do that. But Mrs. B was an old lady. So it didn't occur to anyone to ask her to make that promise.

As you might guess, Mrs. B was no ordinary grandma. Five years after selling the Nebraska Furniture Mart, she bought the land across the street and started another furniture store. Again, she was 95 years old!

She called the new store Mrs. B's Clearance and Factory Outlet. Mrs. B was one of the reasons that everyone shopped at the old store. Everyone loved her. So of course, people started shopping at the new store instead of the one that Warren owned. But Warren was a good sport. He was a big fan of Mrs. B too. He laughed about it and said that it was a good lesson for him. He would not make the mistake of letting the feisty Mrs. B (or anyone else) sell him a business without signing a non-compete clause again.

It only took two years for Mrs. B's new business to become the third biggest carpet store in town. Buying Mrs. B's first business had worked out great for Warren (until she opened a new one). So he was happy to buy her new business as well. There aren't many people who have sold more than one business to Warren Buffet. There's even fewer who have ever outsmarted him. But Rose Blumkin was a special lady.

She lived until she was 104. And even though she was a millionaire, she kept working at the business with her name on it well past 100 years old. She is a wonderful example of what you can get out of life if you are smart, work hard, and if you're always honest and fair.

"I dreamed all my life, since I was six years old. The first dream of mine was to go to America."

- Rose Blumkin

The Most Famous Athlete in the World Was a Runt of a Kid

Lionel Messi recently achieved one of the most glorious feats in all of sports. He and his teammates won the World Cup for their home country of Argentina. He is widely recognized as the greatest soccer player in the world as I write this. That makes him the best in the most popular sport on the planet.

As you might imagine, the poor guy can't go anywhere in his home country without being mobbed by fans. He is Argentina's greatest hero. So it might surprise you to find out what he had to overcome to be the best in the world.

Argentina loves soccer. Most kids play the game there as soon as they can walk. Lionel certainly did, and he was pretty much amazing from the time he first kicked a ball. He had two older brothers and two cousins to play with. His dad coached him on a team when he was only four years old.

After two years had passed, Lionel joined a local soccer club team called Newell's Old Boys. He would play for that club for six years until he was 12. During that time, he scored nearly 500 goals. Lionel was special, and he was special early.

But his parents noticed that he was smaller than all the rest of the boys he played with and against.

They took him to the doctor and found out that there was a problem with their 10-year-old son. Lionel had a growth disorder. He didn't have enough growth hormones in his body to grow normally.

This disorder could keep him from developing like the rest of the boys. If that happened, his dreams of playing professionally would be over. Every night, Lionel needed medicine injected into his legs. The medicine cost $1,000 a month. His family could not afford that. Fortunately, his dad had insurance but it only covered two years of treatment.

When that two years was nearing its end, Lionel's family started to panic. The Newell's Old Boys club said that they would help. What a relief! But they broke their promise. It was an emotional rollercoaster for young Lionel. The professional soccer club in Buenos Aires, Argentina was interested in him but didn't want to pay for his hormone treatment.

A savior did arrive. The soccer club in Barcelona, Spain agreed to sign the young boy. This was in doubt for quite some time because they had never signed anyone so young to a professional contract. Lionel was only 13. And Spain was on the other side of the Atlantic Ocean from Argentina and 6,500 miles away. But they would let him continue to play soccer AND pay for the medicine he needed to grow like a normal boy.

The family made the move. But things weren't easy. Lionel's new club couldn't play him in games that actually mattered because of a transfer rule. This made it hard to fit in with the other players. Lionel was really shy. That didn't help either. He was so shy that the Spanish players thought that he couldn't talk! The boy from Argentina didn't make any friends on his new team.

After a year, Lionel's mom moved back to Argentina with his two brothers and younger sister. It was just Lionel and his dad. This made Lionel even more homesick than he already was. The loneliness was now almost unbearable.

Two significant things happened next that made everything better. He finally finished his expensive growth hormone therapy. The doctors said that it had helped, and he would be just fine. Then when Lionel was 15, he could finally play in regular matches with the Barcelona youth team. He started to make friends with the other players. And everyone started to see what this kid was capable of on the soccer field.

Not only did he lead his team in scoring during his first full season, they were nearly unbeatable. A week before the championship game Lionel got hurt in a game. He broke the cheekbone in his face. Ouch! He could only play in the final if he wore a protective mask.

He got out there and hated it. But if he played without it and got hit in the face, he could be seriously hurt. Lionel yanked it off anyway and threw it off the field. He quickly scored two goals before his coach sent in a substitute for him. The victory was theirs.

From there, he kept getting better and better. By the time he was 19, he was already one of the best players in the world, still playing for Barcelona, the team that had invested in his medical salvation. He wasn't entirely in the clear yet, though.

For nearly two years, Lionel was getting injured a lot. Perhaps related to his years of underdeveloped growth as a boy, his muscles seemed to easily injure which cost him a lot of time. Barcelona would continue to invest in their star player. They put him on a new diet, new training plans, and gave him access to new full-time doctors that would travel with him everywhere.

This worked and kept Lionel playing without injuries for the next four years of his career. This allowed him to truly develop into one of the top players in the sport. He would play for Barcelona for 21 years setting the record for goals ever scored in the Spanish professional league with 474.

Lionel has the record for winning the Ballon d'Or Award for the best soccer player in the world, by winning it an amazing seven times. He has more assists than any player in the history of soccer with 358 and has scored an incredible 814 goals as a professional. And still at the age of 36, he is one of the best players in America's MLS with Inter Miami. But Lionel would tell you that his greatest achievement is finally winning the World Cup for Argentina.

Lionel Messi grew up to become one of the best soccer players in the history of the world. It's an incredible accomplishment, especially for a boy who doctors thought might not grow enough to keep playing the game.

"I always thought I wanted to play professionally, and I always knew that to do that I'd have to make a lot of sacrifices. I made sacrifices by leaving Argentina, leaving my family to start a new life. I changed my friends, my people. Everything. But everything I did, I did for football, to achieve my dream."

- Lionel Messi

Anything Is Possible

Sarah Breedlove was a little different from her siblings when she was born. Sarah was born after the abolishment of slavery, which meant that Sarah was born into freedom. Her parents and siblings had all been born into slavery. This new freedom gave Sarah hope in the possibilities that came with freedom, but she would have to overcome many obstacles to reach her full potential. Sarah would become one of the first Black female millionaires, but it would not be an easy road to success.

Just because she was born free from being a slave didn't mean Sarah didn't have to work. She and her brothers and sisters grew up picking cotton in the fields. Money was tight, and Sarah had to work hard. When she was just 7 years old, both of her parents died, leaving Sarah an orphan. Sarah moved in with her older sister and her husband. Her sister's husband was a mean man. As soon as she was old enough, Sarah got married so she could move away.

Life was happy for a while. Sarah and her husband had a baby named A'Lelia. When her husband died, Sarah needed help. She moved to St. Louis to be close to her brothers. Her brothers all worked as barbers in St. Louis. Sarah got a job doing laundry. It was hard work and didn't pay much money. Most days Sarah only made $1.50 a day. The chemicals in the soap were hard on her hair and skin.

Still, Sarah was hopeful in this new life. She joined a church and met people with big dreams and ideas. These people inspired Sarah. She started looking for new opportunities in her own life.

With the harsh chemicals wreaking havoc on her hair and scalp, Sarah began to search for hair products to repair her damaged hair. She found a product she liked and began to use it and even sell it. But Sarah thought the product could be better. She talked to her brothers about their ideas and solutions to this hair problem.

Sarah moved to Denver, Colorado. There she met her new husband, Charles Joseph Walker. Sarah renamed herself Madam C.J. Walker. With this new name, Sarah reinvented herself. She and her husband spent $1.25 and launched a new hair care product line for Black women. She called it "Madam Walker's Wonderful Hair Grower."

C.J. Walker's new product line was a hit, but she had to hustle to make it a success. She spent a year and a half traveling door to door selling her hair cream. She gave demonstrations in churches and women's meetings. She devised new selling and marketing strategies. Her husband helped her create a mail-order catalog. It turned out that Madam C.J. Walker was quite skilled at marketing. She was clever and seemed to have a knack for big business.

Just a few years later, Madam C.J. Walker opened a factory in Indiana to mass-produce her own hair care and beauty products. She wanted to help other Black women be independent, too. So she started a training program for sales agents who could sell her products and make a commission. She encouraged other women entrepreneurs. She trained them in the best ways to market and sell products. She knew that their success was also her success. Madam C.J. Walker's company employed 40,000 Black men and women throughout America and the Caribbean. From being born just on the other side of slavery to being an extraordinary business leader, Madam C.J. Walker opened doors for many people.

As her business grew, so did her desire to help people. She supported many charities and donated lots of money. Financially she helped build schools, YMCA's, and supported Black organizations. She owned several houses throughout America. When she died, Madam C.J. Walker was said to have a net worth of close to one million dollars. Today, that would be worth nearly eighteen million dollars, but it was a remarkable amount back in the early 1900s. She was the wealthiest Black woman in America! Not bad for a young girl who grew up picking cotton in the fields.

"I had to make my own living and my own opportunity. But I made it! Don't sit down and wait for the opportunities to come. Get up and make them."
- Madam C. J. Walker

A Dream About a Killer Robot
Changed Everything

This story is about a guy who Time Magazine has called one of the top 100 most influential people alive. He's the first person to go by himself down to the bottom of the Mariana Trench, which is the deepest place in the ocean. And he's not even known as an explorer! He's James Cameron, the movie director. His movies have made more than eight billion dollars, which makes James the second most successful movie director of all time.

Interestingly, James had no idea that he would ever be influential or successful at anything. That's what makes his story so interesting. James dropped out of college and worked as a high school janitor and a truck driver. His dad had been really strict. His mom had encouraged him to dabble in art. What James loved more than anything was building things.

James and his friends would build rockets, go-karts, and all kinds of stuff. He also enjoyed drawing and painting. And then when he was 16, he saw a really cool science fiction movie, *2001: A Space Odyssey*. James loved this movie so much that he bought a camera and started filming. He fell in love with it. That's when he got some really good luck.

James' dad would be transferred for work. The family would move from one side of North America to the other. They moved from the Canadian side of Niagara Falls (north of New York) to Los Angeles, California. That's right by Hollywood where most of the movies are made. James was excited.

He graduated high school and went to college but soon dropped out. He got a job as a truck driver and would often have to pull over to the side of the road to write down a cool idea he'd get for a movie. But he was just drifting around not sure what he should do with his life. That's when the *Star Wars* movie came out. James was once again inspired by science fiction movies. He knew that somehow he had to learn how to make movies.

He got to work learning all he could about movie production. Then he started getting jobs working on movies. He learned about special effects and each job he got taught him something new. He kept getting better and better. He was in charge of the special effects on a silly horror movie about killer fish, *Piranha II* when the director suddenly quit. James was promoted and finally had the chance to be a director.

James was stressed and exhausted. He got sick with a fever while he was working on the Piranha movie and had a strange dream. He saw a robot crawling on a battlefield trying to kill him. Sounds scary! When he woke up he started writing it all down. He had his new movie idea.

When James had written out the script for a movie where a robot hitman from the future was trying to kill someone, he was having trouble selling it. Some movie studios were interested but didn't trust this young guy who only directed a weird Piranha movie to do the job. James finally found a studio that was willing to let him direct the movie. But because it was such a risk to hire him, they only bought the movie for one dollar. That's right, they bought it for $1.00! That was just fine with James. All he cared about was getting the chance to direct his very own movie.

Arnold Schwarzenegger was really interested in the movie, and James decided to hire him to play one of the robots who fought in the movie. The movie was *The Terminator*, and it turned out to be a big smash success. James had done it! People loved his movie. He was now a big success, and that success continued. He kept having big hits with other science fiction movie ideas that he had. He was on a roll.

When James directed *Titanic*, it became the most successful movie in history. Years later, he broke his own record with *Avatar*. Interestingly, the ideas for many of his movies kept coming to him when he slept. He would have some crazy dream or nightmare and write it down the next day and put it in a movie.

James Cameron became one of the most successful movie directors in the history of movies. And that's not bad for a truck-driving college dropout who had no idea what to do with his life. It took him a while to realize that he was good enough to chase his dreams.

And his dream started when he was 16. He just needed to start believing in himself. Once he decided that he would go for it, the rest was history.

"There are many talented people who haven't fulfilled their dreams because they over thought it, or they were too cautious, and were unwilling to make the leap of faith."
- James Cameron

This Kid is Unstoppable

This story is as remarkable as it is improbable. Meet my new personal hero, Cornel Hrisca-Munn. Cornel was born in Romania. He was born with a deformed leg and no forearms. His mother screamed when she saw him.

Doctors immediately had him removed from the hospital and sent to a horrible orphanage. He was put in a room with other babies that nobody wanted and left to die. Because the doctors thought he would be dead in a few hours, Cornel wasn't even issued a birth certificate. His parents wanted to get him back but were too poor to do so.

So there he was, a baby without hands in a metal cot on a dirty mattress with a little milk. The conditions in Romanian orphanages at that time were tragic and horrific. Amazingly, Cornel survived for nine months. It's truly incredible that he made it. But this miracle baby was just getting started.

An English woman had driven to the orphanage to deliver much-needed supplies for the orphans who lived there. A doctor showed her this strange baby that desperately needed help.

Doreen Munn was shocked by everything she saw. She went home and told her husband all about it. She couldn't get that poor baby out of her mind. They had to do something. Their local hospital graciously said

that they would treat the baby for free if the Munns adopted it. That was wonderful. But getting this baby to England would not be easy.

It would be over a year before the Munns were able to find and get permission from both the government and Cornel's birth parents. It was also very difficult to convince the British government that they should be allowed to adopt this baby. The Munns already had four children of their own. But Doreen knew that she was Cornel's only hope.

They finally got him eight months later. He was almost a year and a half old. The hospital didn't go back on their promise and got to work. They would need to cut off Cornel's deformed leg. He couldn't use it. The boy was finally getting the medical help that he needed.

Cornel learned English quickly. His new parents fell in love with him right away and could tell that he was very smart. With a loving family, Cornel thrived. Right away, he refused to let anything stop him. He had already survived so much. He learned how to ride a tricycle, and as a 6-year-old, Cornel raised money for another sick Romanian child by going on a 4-mile ride around a park.

There were so many children back in Romania who needed help. Cornel, still without one leg, either forearm, or hands, answered the call by participating in all sorts of fundraisers. He swam in races, he did bike-athons, and even won a poetry competition. He was completely dedicated to helping other disabled and poor children back in Romania.

He taught himself how to play the drums. He learned how to play the guitar. Both of those instruments are hard enough with arms and hands! When Cornel was 14, he went to a band competition with 400 kids all trying to win. He beat almost all of them, finishing in 2nd place.

Next, he started his own band. Cornel became a viral YouTube sensation with his drumming skills. He started his own foundation to raise money for the children of Romania. He was accepted into the highly respected college, Oxford University, and graduated with a master's degree. Today, Cornel works for the prestigious Lloyds Banking Group as a senior manager and remains a professional drummer. Look him up on YouTube! He's an incredible musician.

Cornel's inner drive blows me away. It's more than inspiring. It's astonishing all that he has accomplished. He's a real testament to the power of the human spirit to both succeed against all odds and to help others. But he does deal with something that all disabled people recognize. He doesn't want credit for anything just because he's disabled. He doesn't see himself as being inspiring, he's simply living his life.

He commented about how nice it was to attend the Disability Expo in London. "I can exist (here) without being stared at, commented on, offered awkward help, laughed at, or called 'inspirational' for nothing, shows how exhausting just existing as disabled can be. I've not been called 'amazing' once today, it's bliss!"

"I'm at my most confident performing in front of people."
- Cornel Hrisca-Munn

He Was Just a Poor Farm Boy

There was a 12-year-old on a cold farm in Michigan, messing with a watch that his dad had given him. He would take it apart and put it back together. He liked seeing how the watch worked on the inside. The little gears were so interesting. It was around this time that the boy saw what was called a "road engine." The year was 1875, and cars had not been invented yet. But this kid watched in amazement as he saw this weird thing move down the road on its own! It was the first vehicle that he had ever seen that didn't need horses to pull it. This farm kid would grow up and change the world.

It was only a year later that Henry Ford's mom died. He was 13. He had two younger sisters and two younger brothers. Both sets of Henry's grandparents had come to the United States to find a better life. He was the grandson of immigrants, and farming was tough. His mom had lost both of her parents when she was young and was adopted by some nice neighbors. Henry's parents didn't have much. They had to work really hard to grow food and survive the Michigan winters.

Henry loved his mom very much, so it was really painful and sad to be forced to live without her. Henry's dad worked hard so that his son could take over his farm someday, but Henry had other plans. He didn't like farming much. He later said, "I never had

any particular love for the farm-it was the mother on the farm I loved."

When Henry was 16, he went to Detroit, the big city. There, he became an apprentice working with machine tools. He did this for several years and learned a lot before moving back to the family farm to help out. His dad had gotten a Westinghouse steam engine to make power for their farm machinery. Lots of farms were getting these new things. Henry got really good at working on them and was even hired by the Westinghouse company to work on their steam engines.

In another couple of years, he was building his own engine. Then he was hired away from the farm again back to Detroit by a big electric company where he worked as an engineer. Henry kept building in his free time. He built cars in his garage at home. They didn't look like the cars you ride in today. Henry's were powered by gas, though they ran on bicycle tires.

Finally, Henry decided that he was ready to start his own car company. That was exciting and brave! But the company had trouble making cars as good as Henry wanted and making them cheap enough for people to afford. So that company failed. But Henry tried again and named a new company after himself, the Henry Ford Company. But that one didn't work out either, and Henry left it even though he had named it after himself. The company renamed itself Cadillac and still makes cars today.

Henry could not stop making cars or starting new companies to do it. He kept going. He really wanted to make a car that everyone could afford, and he finally did it with a car he called the Model T. It was a huge hit and quickly became the biggest car company in the country. Henry's new company, the Ford Motor Company, made and sold more than 15 million Model T cars.

Henry became famous not only for selling so many cars but also for paying his workers more than any other company in the world. This brought him all the best mechanics and workers from all of the other car companies. Henry is also the guy who invented weekends. What? People were used to working six days a week. But he decided that they needed another day to relax with their families and started opening his factories for only five days a week. This is the reason that you go to school for five days instead of six every week. Thank you, Henry Ford!

Henry is also credited with this quote, "Whether you think you can, or you think you can't, you're right."

I personally think that this is one of the most important quotes of all time. It is super important to believe that you can do something...before you can do it. But it's hard to believe in ourselves sometimes, isn't it? But we should always try because only then can we really achieve our biggest dreams.

Henry was once asked if he ever worried about things going wrong. To that, he said, "You must never, even for a second, let yourself think that you can fail. Our first principle is that failure is impossible. You may not get what you're trying to do right the first time or the second time or the tenth time or the 100th time, but if you shut out of your mind the possibility of being licked, then you are bound to win."

In those days, "licked" meant getting beat. And that attitude is how a young farm kid who really missed his mom grew up to change the world by bringing cars to millions of people.

"There is no man living who isn't capable of doing more than he thinks he can do."

- Henry Ford

16-Year-Old Homeless Dropout Hits It Big

He had to make it. He just had to. But for now, he found himself sleeping by a heating duct that kicked out warm air from inside Buckingham Palace. This was the London palace where the Queen of England lived. But this kid? He wasn't so lucky. Little did he know that he would one day perform to a crowd of thousands just a few yards from where he was shivering.

Ed Sheeran has always been talented. When he was 4, you could catch him singing with his church choir. He was that good even at just 4 years old. He got a guitar when he was 11 and learned how to play. That's when he started writing his own songs. When Ed was 13, his classmates voted him "most likely to become famous." He was a talented kid. But that doesn't mean he didn't get bullied. He says that's one of the reasons he turned to music. It was the only thing that made him happy.

Ed had recorded his own album by the time he was 13. (No wonder his classmates knew he was going places.) He would sell it to people on the streets of his town and perform his songs anywhere he could. That summer, he went to stay in London where he figured he could get paid to sing. And he did. A year later he had a second album.

Unfortunately, his home life wasn't great. When Ed was 16, he'd had enough. He left. He dropped out of school and would live on the streets if he had to. And that's exactly what he did for almost three years. It's very dangerous to be homeless and survive by living on the streets, especially for a teenager. Please don't ever consider doing that. But luckily, Ed made it through those years without anything bad happening to him. He had to be smart though.

The subway trains would start running at five in the morning. He would stay up all night, and then hop on the subway and sleep. He felt safe that way. Lots of times he could sleep on a friend's floor. But there were lots of nights on the subway and under archways in the city too. All the while, he kept performing and writing songs. Ed worked extremely hard. During one year of being homeless, he did more than 300 live performances. People were starting to notice.

When Ed was 19, he got his big break. A famous rapper, Example, saw one of Ed's songs on YouTube and invited him to go on his tour with him and be the opening act. Ed had been uploading his songs onto the internet for years and years. This chance to perform with Example was great for Ed and led to more and more attention and new fans. He recorded three new albums that year as well. He lived and breathed music. He always had.

Ed was still an independent musician. He did not have a contract with any music labels. He decided to take his chance on making it in the United States. He flew to Los Angeles with not much more than hope. Taking chances and betting on himself was nothing new for Ed. He happened to play a gig and was seen by the famous actor, Jamie Foxx. Jamie was impressed, and when he heard that Ed had nowhere to stay, he invited him to sleep on his couch and stay in his house. Jamie just so happened to have a recording studio in his house. With Jamie's help, Ed got more and more attention. There was still no record contract though.

Amazingly, that next year, one of Ed's albums made it to the number two most downloaded album on iTunes! There was no advertising for it and no big company behind it. It was just some kid from England with a big dream, but boy did it catch on. Now, all the record companies wanted to sign him. He was soon winning all the awards in music. He had made it. And soon after, at 21 years old, he performed in front of Buckingham Palace and shook hands with the Queen of England in an amazing moment for the young singer. He could still see the archway nearby that he huddled in for warmth just a few years earlier. Now, he was the star of the show.

Ed Sheeran was homeless for two and a half years as he struggled to make it in the music business. It took an incredible amount of determination and believing in himself to not quit. He has since sold more than 150 million albums, which makes him one of the most successful singers in the history of music. He is one of the most loved singers in the world and does a lot of great charity work to help people who don't have much and struggle to survive just as he used to. To say that his story is inspiring falls short. It's more than that. It's truly remarkable what he has accomplished.

"I think to be successful at anything you have to put in a (heck) of a lot of effort. Pick your battles. I picked music, put in a lot of effort, and it's worked."

- Ed Sheeran

Kid from the Housing Projects Builds a $115 BILLION Dollar Company?

Growing up in the housing projects of Brooklyn, New York, makes kids really tough. It's hard when your family is worried every single day about getting food. Fortunately, Howard was tough. He had to be.

Howard's parents both dropped out of high school, and his dad was working as a truck driver. The street-tough kid loved sports. He'd play anything. And he kept playing. He did well as a high schooler and was offered a chance at a football scholarship at a small school, Northern Michigan University. He would be the first person from his family to go to college.

When Howard got to the school that was miles and miles from where he grew up, things didn't go so well. He stepped onto the football practice fields and quickly realized that he was not good enough to play for the team. The coaches saw it too. He would have to pay for college somehow.

He quickly took any job he could and even started selling his blood at blood drives for some money. He also got all the student loans that he could from the college. And four years later, he was a college graduate. He had made it work, and he had done it. Now what?

He stayed in Michigan and got a job working at a ski resort. Then he moved back to New York and got a sales job. He sold printers for a few years and was approached by a Swedish company that made kitchen appliances. They wanted Howard to be in charge of growing their business for coffee makers in the United States. He took the job.

Howard noticed that he was getting lots of orders from a small company in Seattle, Washington. This company was called Starbucks. He thought that he'd better fly out there and meet them because they were becoming good customers. Starbucks was just a small company at this time, and all they sold were coffee beans, not hot coffee like they do today. They hired Howard to try and grow their business.

Howard worked for them for a couple of years, but that hadn't gone too well. He had the idea that they should start selling hot cups of coffee instead of just the beans for people to use at home. But the Starbucks owners had little interest in opening coffee shops. They liked their business just the way it was. They couldn't see Howard's big vision. So Howard quit and started his own coffee shop. But he was still friendly with the Starbucks owners, and they invested in his new business.

And that was good because he needed a lot of money to start a coffee shop. He asked everyone he could think of to invest in his new idea. 217 people said no. That's a lot of rejection! But 25 people had agreed to give him some money, and he was able to open up his coffee shop. He was on his way. He called his new store, Il Giornale, which was Italian. And it did well.

In just two years, he bought Starbucks! Howard was now in charge and could do what he wanted. And what Howard wanted was to go big, really big. He wanted a Starbucks store in every city in the United States. The company started to grow really fast. Four years later they made Starbucks available on the stock market for anyone to be able to invest in them. This was a big success and gave the company $270 million to keep growing.

When Howard finally retired from Starbucks, he had grown the company from 11 stores in Seattle, all the way up to 28,000 stores all over the world. That's a lot of coffee! The people who live back in the housing project that he grew up in are really proud of him. Howard Schultz's success means that it doesn't matter where you're born or how much money your family has when you're a kid. It means that anyone, no matter how poor you might be, can be a big success. The company that Howard built is now worth $115 billion, and Howard no longer worries about money like he did when he was a kid.

"I am convinced that most people can achieve their dreams and beyond if they have the determination to keep trying."
- Howard Schultz

My Hand Exploded? Oh Well...

Sometimes a person is so obsessed with a goal or a dream that it doesn't matter what stands in their way. This is the unbelievable story of a Hungarian sharpshooter.

Kàroly Takàcs was a sergeant in the Hungarian military, and he was incredibly talented at marksmanship, especially when he had a pistol in his hand. He would calmly place his feet, point the pistol at the target, breathe out, pull the trigger, and fire. Then he would smile as he saw a small hole in exactly the center of whatever he was aiming at.

Kàroly was really, really good. He wanted to go to the Olympics. In 1936, Hungary only allowed its commissioned officers to compete at the Olympics. Kàroly was just a sergeant, but Hungary removed that restriction after the 1936 Olympics. Maybe their commissioned officers didn't win any medals! This meant that Kàroly was free to start training with a chance to go represent his country at the Olympics.

Two years before the next Olympics, disaster struck. Kàroly was with his army unit training with grenades. The grenade that Kàroly had was defective. It blew up when it shouldn't have. Kàroly was right-handed and used that hand to shoot, write, and do just about everything, including throwing grenades. The bad grenade exploded while he was still holding it, and poor

Kàroly lost his right hand and part of his arm. That must have been really painful. He was lucky just to be alive after that kind of accident.

His friends were all really sad for him. His dream of going to the Olympics was certainly over. If you're right-handed, have you tried writing with your left hand? It's terrible! The same is true for shooting a gun. Even the best shooters aren't very good when they use their nondominant hand. But Kàroly wasn't so sure that his dream was done. Even though it wouldn't occur to most of us that we still have a chance, Kàroly wasn't like most people.

When he got out of the hospital, he wanted to know if he could shoot with his left hand. In case he couldn't, he tried it without anyone else watching. His worst fears were true. He was terrible. Kàroly was used to hitting the bullseye in the center of the target every time he shot with his right hand. But with his left? He was shooting bullets all over the place. It was a good thing that nobody else was there to see it.

There was one person who still believed in Kàroly. It was his shooting coach, Laszlo. Laszlo told Kàroly that he could do this. That helped Kàroly start to believe it, too. He worked and he worked and he worked. All Kàroly did in his free time was shoot his pistol at targets. And slowly he got better. But he didn't have much time, and this was pretty much like someone who had never shot a gun before thinking that they could make it to the Olympics. Kàroly knew that his only chance was to practice as much as he possibly could. Did Hungary even have enough bullets? He must have shot a million of them in the short time that he had.

Hungary had a shooting tournament to decide who they would send to the Olympics. They would only send the very best. The other shooters were surprised to see Kàroly there. They all felt sorry for him. Wait, you're competing? Some of them probably thought that he had gone crazy and felt even sorrier for him. Everyone there watched closely as he walked up to the firing line. Nobody made a sound. And nobody could believe their eyes as Kàroly calmly hit bullseye after bullseye and won the tournament with ease. It was an incredible accomplishment. Kàroly would finally compete at the Olympics! And then disaster struck yet again.

The 1940 Olympics were canceled. What? World War II had broken out. It was just one more horrible obstacle that Kàroly would have to overcome. He had already come this far. It was a bitter disappointment, but he thought that he could wait another four years. But four years later, the war was still raging and the next Olympics was canceled too. Can you imagine how Kàroly must have felt? The disappointment must have been overwhelming. He had worked so hard. And now he had to wait another four years?

When the 1948 Olympics finally came around, Kàroly was 38 years old. For sharpshooters, that was old. He would be at a disadvantage compared to the better eyes of the younger shooters. Oh, and he was also shooting with his left hand, let's not forget that disadvantage either. But this was Kàroly's destiny. He won gold. He did it! He was officially the best sharpshooter in the entire world with his left hand.

And four years later, he did it again at the age of 42. That was even crazier for a guy at that age to win this kind of competition. Kàroly was robbed not only of his right hand but also three chances at Olympic glory. None of that mattered. His determination was stronger than exploding grenades, his aging eyes, and even stronger than a world war. And that is the remarkable story of Kàroly Takàcs, the man who refused to let anything stand in the way of becoming a champion.

"I didn't come to watch, I came to compete."

- Károly Takács

"You Sound like a Goat."

You might be forgiven for thinking that a little girl who lived in a little town in the South American country of Colombia probably wouldn't grow up to become "one of the most influential female artists of the 21st century." Not many other people believed in her either. But now, there is a huge statue of her in that little Colombian town. Pretty cool!

Her name is Shakira, and she would take the world by storm with her unique style of music. But as with all of our heroes in this book, nothing would come easy for Shakira. She had a lot of talent for a young kid. She was just 4 years old when she wrote her first poem. She kept writing poems and eventually those poems turned into songs.

She was also 4 when she discovered another big influence in her life. Her dad took her to a restaurant where someone was playing traditional belly dancer music. Four-year-old Shakira loved it and started dancing and wiggling like crazy...on the table! It was cute and funny. From that moment on, she knew that she wanted to be on stage as a performer.

She also loved to sing. She sang all the time. So naturally, she tried out for the 2nd-grade choir at her school. Even though she was only in the 2nd grade, the choir teacher said something really mean. She said that she couldn't be in the choir. And the reason was

(the teacher actually said this) that poor little Shakira sounded "like a goat." Ouch! That's really harsh.

It was around then that Shakira wrote her first song. She was 8 years old. Apparently, she didn't mind that the foolish teacher thought that she sounded like a goat. Shakira had her own style. She also still enjoyed belly dancing and was always learning new dances and showing them off at school. (That mean choir teacher probably didn't like that either.)

It was also when Shakira was 8 that her dad took her to see the children in town who didn't have a mom or dad to take care of them. He wanted Shakira to be grateful for everything that she had. Shakira was grateful. And she never forgot those orphans. She really believed in herself and thought, "One day I'm going to help these kids when I become a famous artist."

She started to get popular when she was between 10 and 13 years old by performing around town. A local producer saw her and thought that she was really talented and decided to help her. He played her music for an important music businessman with Sony Records. But that man thought that the future "Queen of Latin Music" was "a lost cause." He didn't hear anything special.

The local producer didn't care. He believed in Shakira as much as she believed in herself. So he set up another audition with other businesspeople from Sony. They liked her much better and signed her up for a music deal!

Unfortunately, that first album was a total flop. She recorded it when she was 13 and she had written all of the songs. After it failed, she went down to Chile to compete in a song competition. She came in 3rd place. Not bad! There was one judge who thought she should have won. His name was Ricky Martin. Ricky was only 20 years old, but he would become a big singing star himself soon.

Shakira's second album was also a flop. But that really wasn't so bad considering how young she was. She hadn't even graduated high school yet! Sony wasn't sure that they would pay her to do a third album. But a new song she sang started to get popular on the radio and that changed their minds. This would be her last chance with Sony.

The third album exploded in popularity. It had six top hits both in Latin America and the United States as well. Shakira was on her way to stardom. But all of these popular songs were in Spanish. Shakira didn't know how to speak or sing in English yet. Another popular singer took an interest in her and helped her to learn. Her name was Gloria Estefan.

Shakira's first English language album sold 200,000 copies in the first week after it was released. Wow! That's not bad for a girl who sounded like a goat when she sang, is it? There were still people who didn't like her music though. The popular Rolling Stone magazine said "she sounds downright silly." But there were millions of fans who disagreed.

It's okay to be different. If you are, there are often people who won't like you because you have your own new style. They're used to something else. But if you are different, you have a special chance at success because of that uniqueness! Shakira was very different. She would yodel in her songs and mix that with belly dancing. Nobody had ever done that in the history of music.

Fans couldn't get enough, and Shakira went on to be one of the most popular singers of all time by selling more than 75 million albums. And remember those orphan children that Shakira was shown when she was 8? She sure did. She stayed true to the promise she made herself all those years ago. She started a charity that has fed and educated thousands and thousands of orphans in Colombia. Her charity work has won her lots of awards and the respect of the world. It's not only okay to be different, but being different can be a superpower and a big advantage. It was for Shakira.

"In this life, to earn your place you have to fight for it."
- Shakira

The Slave Who Became a
Spokesperson for Freedom

Can you imagine what it would be like to not only have no idea how old you are, but not know what day your birthday is? That would be weird, but certainly not the worst thing about growing up as a slave. American slavery was brutal and one of history's great injustices.

As a young boy, Frederick Douglass realized the importance of learning to read. Frederick was a slave. He lived in the early 1800s in Baltimore, Maryland. One of his owners started to teach him the alphabet when he was 12 but stopped when her husband decided that was a bad idea. Why was that a bad idea? The reason would change everything for Frederick.

The man who owned Frederick told his wife that learning to read would make a slave want to be free. When Frederick heard this, he knew that the first step for him would be this power of literacy. He became determined to learn it because that had to be the path toward freedom. But he had to be careful. His owners would take any newspaper or book that he had snuck into the house away from him.

Frederick had to teach himself to read in secret. Anytime he was out of the house, he would learn all he could from White children who weren't slaves and did

know how to read. And once he had learned how to read, he learned writing by watching carpenters write down words on the wood they were working with at the shipyard that he worked at.

You have to be very determined to learn reading and writing that way. He didn't have school teachers or even paper, pencils, or pens. He used lumps of chalk on concrete or wooden fences. It took Frederick seven years to learn reading and writing in this way. Then, he started teaching other slaves who wanted to learn. On Sundays, slaves from all around would come and learn from Frederick in secret. Frederick knew that it wasn't enough for one slave to learn this power, but that it would help everyone.

Frederick was 16 now and was punished for learning how to read and write. He was beaten badly. And he was beaten often. Finally, he had enough and fought back. And instead of being killed, he was left alone. But Frederick knew that he had to escape. He was finally able to escape slavery by sneaking onto a train bound for New York. He disguised himself as a free Black sailor with fake identification papers. He had to get on and off several trains and eventually a steamboat carried him up the Delaware River to Philadelphia, and to freedom.

He became a preacher, and that helped him get good at speaking in front of others and giving speeches. He wrote the story of his life and had it published. This Black man being able to write so powerfully undermined the false idea that lots of people believed, that Black people were not as smart as White people. That book made him famous, and people flocked to hear him speak about the injustice of slavery.

Frederick published his own newspaper and helped hundreds and hundreds of escaped slaves. He was a powerful figure in the abolitionist movement. This was the movement to end slavery in the United States. Frederick was also a key figure in the struggle for more rights for women. Eventually, he became the first Black man nominated to run for the office of Vice President.

Frederick Douglass is universally thought of as one of the most influential African Americans of the 19th century. He was appointed to many top offices in the country and was often the first Black person to hold those offices and served five different Presidents. He served as a US Marshal for Washington DC, the Recorder of Deeds for Washington DC, and a diplomat as the Minister Resident and Consul General to Haiti.

This is a remarkable level of achievement for a man who grew up as a slave. As a child, Frederick slept on a dirt floor, without parents, was fed scraps of food and nearly starved, and had to leave his feet in the ashes of a fire so he wouldn't freeze at night. Not many had it worse than Frederick Douglass did when he was a kid. But because of his determination, he rose to a position of prominence and always worked to help others. He overcame more hardship than any of us can imagine and refused to let it stop him working for justice and the rights of people everywhere.

"I prefer to be true to myself, even at the hazard of incurring the ridicule of others, rather than to be false, and to incur my own abhorrence."

- Frederick Douglass

8th Grade Dropout Street Boxer Becomes a Billionaire

This story is wild and full of adventure. It has a little bit of everything, from boxers to fighter pilots. You're about to embark on an epic journey that was the life of Kerkor Kerkorian. That's quite a name, isn't it? I bet you've never heard of him. Let's dive in.

Kerkor's parents had to escape war and violence in their homeland of Armenia. They moved to California. Kerkor's father came to the United States with nothing and became wealthy selling raisins. He owned more than a thousand acres for growing grapes but lost everything during a recession when many businesses failed. The family moved to Los Angeles, once again, with nothing.

Kerkor was the youngest of four and started going by the name Kirk to sound more American. He was just 9 years old but had to work. He was a newspaper boy on the streets of Los Angeles. The family had to move around a lot, and Kirk was always getting into fights. He was a tough little kid, and that's good because he had to be.

He once got beat up by a street bully. He kept going back to fight him each day for another three or four days. Kirk kept getting beat up each time. By the last time, even though Kirk still lost the fight, the

bully didn't want to keep fighting this determined kid, and the two became friends. That refusal to give up would serve Kirk well throughout his life.

Kirk kept getting kicked out of schools for all of his fighting. Finally, he decided that he had enough of school and quit when he was in the 8th grade. He took any job he could find. Kirk lied about his age and got a job building roads in the California mountains. He also discovered that he could buy old cars, fix them up, and then sell them for a profit. After all that street fighting he did as a kid, it made sense to make money as a boxer. When Kirk was 20 years old, he earned the nickname "Rifle Right Kerkorian" for his mean right-handed punch. Kirk went 33-4 and never once got knocked out.

The year was now 1939, and Kirk got a job putting heaters inside houses. This is where he met a former navy pilot who got him interested in flying. Kirk loved it so much that he soon forgot all about boxing. He scrimped and saved for flying lessons and saved money by not renting a parachute when he flew! He moved to a ranch in the desert and cleaned up after the hogs in the barn for free flying lessons. In six months, he got a pilot's license. Kirk could really fly.

He became a flying teacher, and then World War II started. Kirk wanted to help but was an 8th grade dropout. A friend got him a fake high school diploma, and he was able to help in the war effort. Rather than join the air force, he flew as a non-soldier. Canada needed pilots to fly warplanes over to Europe to join in the fight. These were extremely dangerous missions. Only one out of every four planes made it to England. Most of the pilots attempting that flight were never seen again. This flight was so dangerous because you needed the right tailwinds to help you cross over the Atlantic Ocean, as the planes didn't have enough gas to make it on their own! You had to be really good to make it across safely. Kirk accomplished it a remarkable 33 times.

Kirk then opened up his own flight school. He continued buying bigger and better planes and selling off the less useful ones. He made good money selling the flight school he started. One time he found a good deal on a bunch of big planes that were stranded in Hawaii without gas tanks big enough to make the flight to California. Kirk was the perfect guy for this mission after his WWII experience. But he almost didn't make it. His family thought he was dead. He threw everything out of the plane as they were going down to use less gas, and they just barely made it. After getting those planes to California, he was able to sell them for much more than he paid for them.

Kirk kept buying planes for cheap, then fixing them up and making a good profit on them. He loved making deals. He was making really good money now and had his own small private airline. He would sell that airline for 150 million dollars. He was also making land deals now in Las Vegas before that city grew into the big tourist city that it is today. Kirk rarely made a bad deal. He had a great reputation for being honest and fair. Not only that but every investment he made seemed to make lots and lots of money. He rented land to big casinos, and even bought some. And then he did it. He built the biggest casino in the world. He called it The International.

Elvis Presley started performing there, and Kirk had lots of famous friends now. Movie stars, singers, everyone wanted to be his friend. He managed to make another great deal through lots of hard work and bought a big movie studio called MGM. He built another huge casino, and the movie studio started to turn a profit. He bought more and more companies, and they were all great investments. He even bought a car company (Chrysler) and made billions on that deal. Kirk had made so much money that when a terrible earthquake hit his homeland of Armenia, he secretly gave more than 1 billion dollars to help the people there rebuild and have food and shelter. It was only years later that his generosity became public, and he became a hero to the Armenian people.

Kirk never stopped making deals or helping people with his generosity. He left most of his fortune to charity. His company became the largest and most important resort company in the world. It's called MGM Resorts International and is worth billions of dollars and provides thousands and thousands of jobs. And it all came from a kid who had to work and fight on the streets of Los Angeles in the 1930s who dropped out of school in the 8th grade. That makes Kirk Kerkorian's achievements truly inspiring.

"You have to ask a lot of questions and listen to people, but eventually, you have to go by your own instincts."

- Kirk Kerkorian

"The Wand Chooses the Wizard."

You've probably read the Harry Potter books or at least seen the movies. They're amazing. It might surprise you to know how difficult it was to get those books published. And that wasn't the half of it. Real life can be stranger than fiction.

The Harry Potter series was written by J.K. Rowling. Her real name is Joanne. And even though she didn't grow up as badly as her character Harry did (living in a closet under the stairs with the Dursleys), she went through incredible difficulty in her life.

Joanne's family was poor. They didn't really understand her. She loved writing. She wrote her very first story when she was only 6 years old. It was about a rabbit who got sick, and all its friends came to check on it. How cute! Joanne was a writer from the very beginning. And her big dream was to do it for a living.

But her parents didn't think that was possible. They didn't have much money and had grown up that way themselves. They thought that the only way to make money was from working really hard in jobs that weren't much fun. They didn't think that Joanne's dream of being a writer was possible, so they discouraged her.

That made Joanne stop talking about it. When she was 9, she had a really mean teacher. This teacher yelled a lot and embarrassed the kids when they didn't do well in class. Joanne remembers being bad at math.

Her teacher called her a dunce and made her sit in a special section for dunces. (Dunce means idiot or dummy.) That teacher sure didn't think much of Joanne. Lots of other people didn't either.

Joanne spent a lot of time in her daydreams when she was young. She wasn't thought of as being cool or pretty. When she wasn't being bullied by other kids, she spent most of her time reading books or writing her own stories. She did this more and more as her home life became difficult.

Joanne's dad seemed to wish that he had boys instead of daughters. And then Joanne's mom got sick. She had gotten a disease called multiple sclerosis, which made her feel terrible and need lots of help. That made things hard on everyone.

When Joanne was ready to go to college she still wanted more than anything to be a writer. But her parents thought that was silly and pressured her into studying something more realistic. She studied French to make them happy and got jobs as a secretary. But she didn't like those jobs after college. She was always writing her own stories instead, which got her in trouble with her bosses and even got her fired!

Then Joanne had a day that changed everything. She was on a long train ride, but there was a problem. The train was stuck for four hours. Joanne didn't have a pen or a paper, but an idea was born. Three book characters appeared in her mind. They were Harry, Hermione, and Ron, the three heroes of the Harry Potter books. For hours, Joanne sat thinking about them and thinking of adventures that they might have. Maybe this is why the characters always rode a train to Hogwarts?

These characters were lots of fun, and Joanne enjoyed writing about them. But then more hardship would come. Her marriage fell apart, and her husband threw her out with her baby. She had no job and a baby to take care of. She went on welfare (which is when the government gives you money to help you if you don't have any), but even then she sometimes didn't have money for food. She would feed the baby, but not have enough left for herself. This made Joanne really sad and depressed. She felt like a failure.

She finally got the first Harry Potter book written. It had taken her five years. As unbelievable as it might sound, nobody liked it! Big publishers weren't impressed and didn't think that it would sell. They didn't think that kids would be interested in it. They probably should have asked some kids! Joanne had to deal with rejection after rejection. Finally, a small publisher decided to take a chance on her and gave a small amount of money. They gave her $2,500. At the time it felt like a million dollars. Joanne was still broke and had hardly any money. But that wouldn't last for much longer.

You can guess the rest of the story. It didn't happen overnight, but kids loved Harry Potter. It became more and more popular. It happened slowly at first, and then it seemed like everyone was talking about it. When the first movie finally came out, it made a billion dollars. It was a smash hit. Joanne was finally the famous author that she had dreamed of when she was a small child. At one point, she actually had more than one billion dollars! That's more money than most people can imagine. She didn't have that much money for long because she gives so much of it away to people who really need it, like she used to. Joanne has given away hundreds of millions of dollars to help people in need.

Joanne is actually the first person to make a billion dollars from writing books. No author has ever been so successful. More than 600 million copies of the Harry Potter books have been sold all over the world. In the beginning, her own publisher had told Joanne that she would never make any money by writing children's books and to get a job. It's a good thing she kept believing! Can you imagine a world without Harry Potter?

"Don't let the muggles get you down."
- J.K. Rowling

YOUR REVIEW

What if I told you that just one minute out of your life could bring joy and jubilation to everyone working at a kids book company?

What am I yapping about? I'm talking about leaving this book a review.

I promise you, we take them **VERY seriously**. Don't believe me?

Each time right after someone just like you leaves this book a review, a little siren goes off right here in our office. And when it does we all pump our fists with pure happiness.

A disco ball pops out of the ceiling, flashing lights come on...it's party time!

Roger, our marketing guy, always and I mean always, starts flossing like a crazy person and keeps it up for awhile. He's pretty good at it. (It's a silly dance he does, not cleaning his teeth)

Sarah, our office manager, runs outside and gives everyone up and down the street high fives. She's always out of breath when she comes back but it's worth it!

Our editors work up in the loft and when they hear the review siren, they all jump into the swirly slide and ride down into a giant pit of marshmallows where they roll around and make marshmallow angels. (It's a little weird, but tons of fun)

So reviews are a pretty big deal for us.

It means a lot and helps others just like you who also might enjoy this book, find it too.

You're the best!
From all of us goofballs at Big Dreams Kids Books

Made in United States
North Haven, CT
14 December 2023

45807766R00075